GW01230224

Bob's Ocean

by Robert Lund

Illustrated by Juliet Ali

© ℗ 2023 Robert Lund

All rights reserved. No portion of this book may be reproduced in any form without written permission from the publisher or author, except as permitted by U.S. copyright law.

ISBN: 979-8-9893412-0-7 (eBook)
ISBN: 979-8-9893412-1-4 (Paperback)
ISBN: 979-8-9893412-2-1 (Hardcover)

Library of Congress Control Number: 2023920782
City of Publication: Honolulu, HI

Illustrated by Juliet Ali
Astryd Design, Inc.

www.robertlundmusic.com

To my guardian angel,

Zena

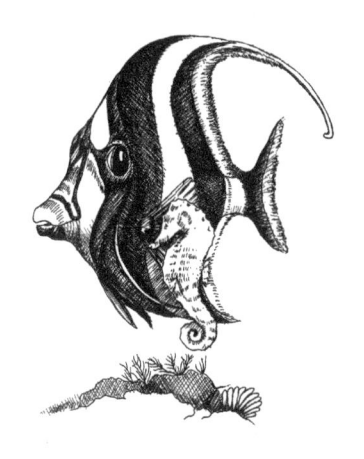

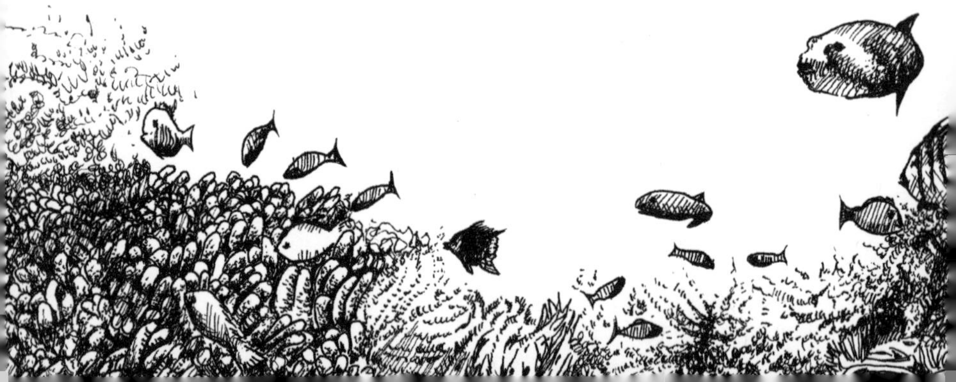

Knowledge: Justified True Belief
- Plato

Ask, and ye shall receive.
- John 16:24 KJV

Once upon a time, there was a fish called Bob.

Every morning, during the week,
Bob woke up and got ready for work.

He usually grabbed a bite to eat on his way to the office where he worked through the morning. At around noon he would have lunch with his buddy Mike and they would talk.

Often their conversation turned to one of their favorite topics - The Ocean. Mike was convinced the Ocean didn't exist while Bob, on the other fin, wasn't sure.

They would talk until it was time to go back to work.

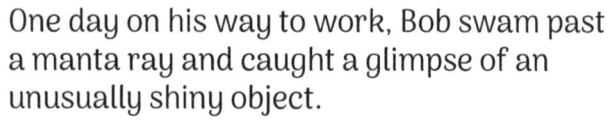

One day on his way to work, Bob swam past a manta ray and caught a glimpse of an unusually shiny object.

He swam up to the object and noticed his favorite food dangling from it. He hadn't eaten yet so he decided to take a bite.

All of a sudden he felt a sharp pain in his mouth, a pain the likes of which he had never felt before.

At first Bob wondered what had happened, but then he realized that the shiny object was now stuck in his mouth.

A feeling of fear overwhelmed him.

Bob swam furiously hoping to remove the object from his mouth. He thrashed and thrashed about but no matter what he did he couldn't dislodge the object.

The feeling of fear grew more intense.

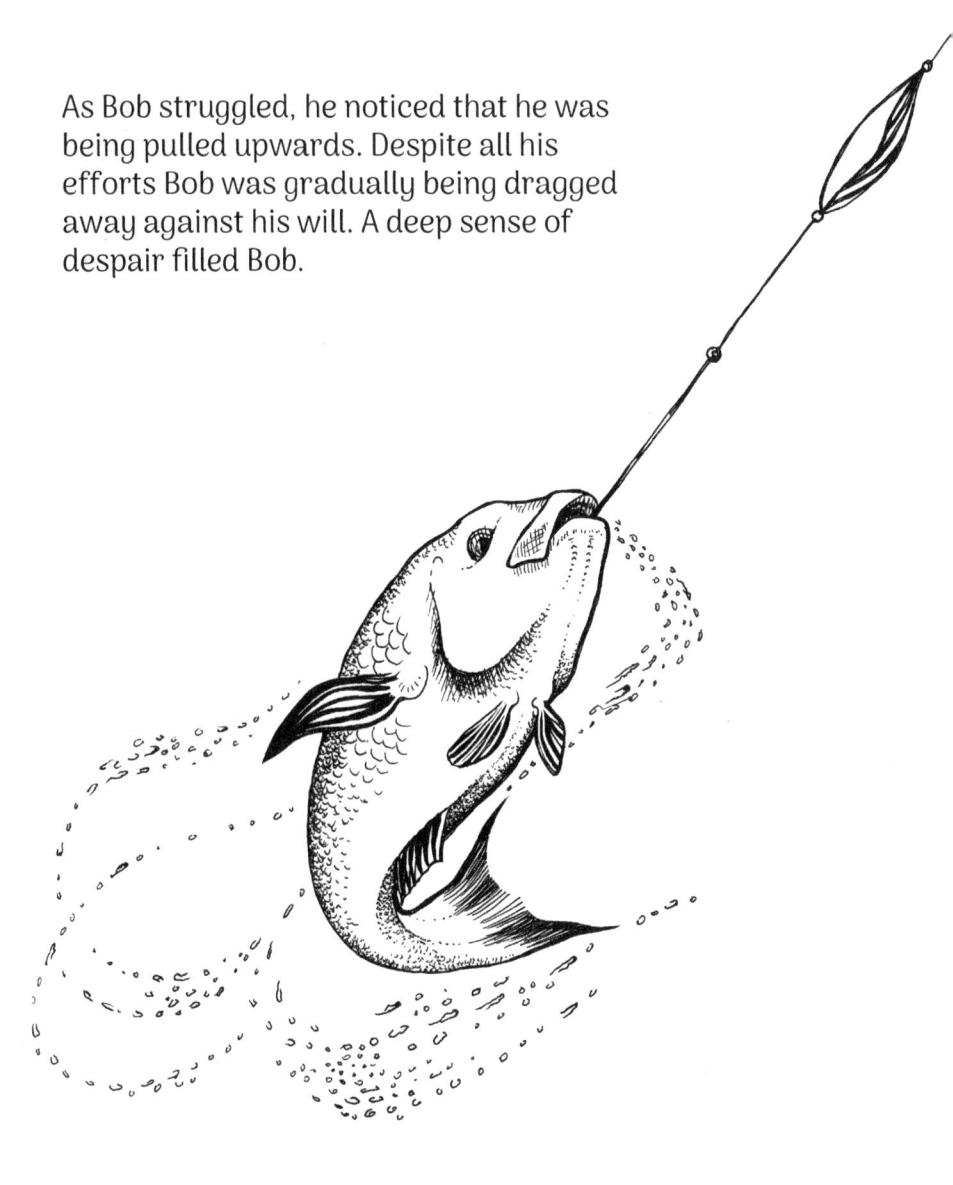

As Bob struggled, he noticed that he was being pulled upwards. Despite all his efforts Bob was gradually being dragged away against his will. A deep sense of despair filled Bob.

For what seemed like an eternity Bob wrestled to free himself. He fought and fought until he could fight no more.

He had all but given up hope.

All of a sudden Bob felt a most unusual sensation. His scales felt strange, his body felt heavy and he was having great difficulty breathing.

Nothing looked or felt the same.

The next thing he knew he was on his side. He couldn't swim and he couldn't breathe. Bob had never known such fear and despair in all his life.

Bob felt like he was going to die.

Just then, Bob felt some pressure on his body and he winced as the object was removed from his mouth.

He felt weightless and heavy all at once.

Then something struck the side of his body.

13

Suddenly Bob felt a familiar sensation. He no longer felt so strange. He could swim and breathe again.

With each passing moment Bob felt better. The feeling of fear and despair slowly disappeared. Bob sighed a deep sigh of relief.

Bob swam home quickly, anxious to share what had happened to him.

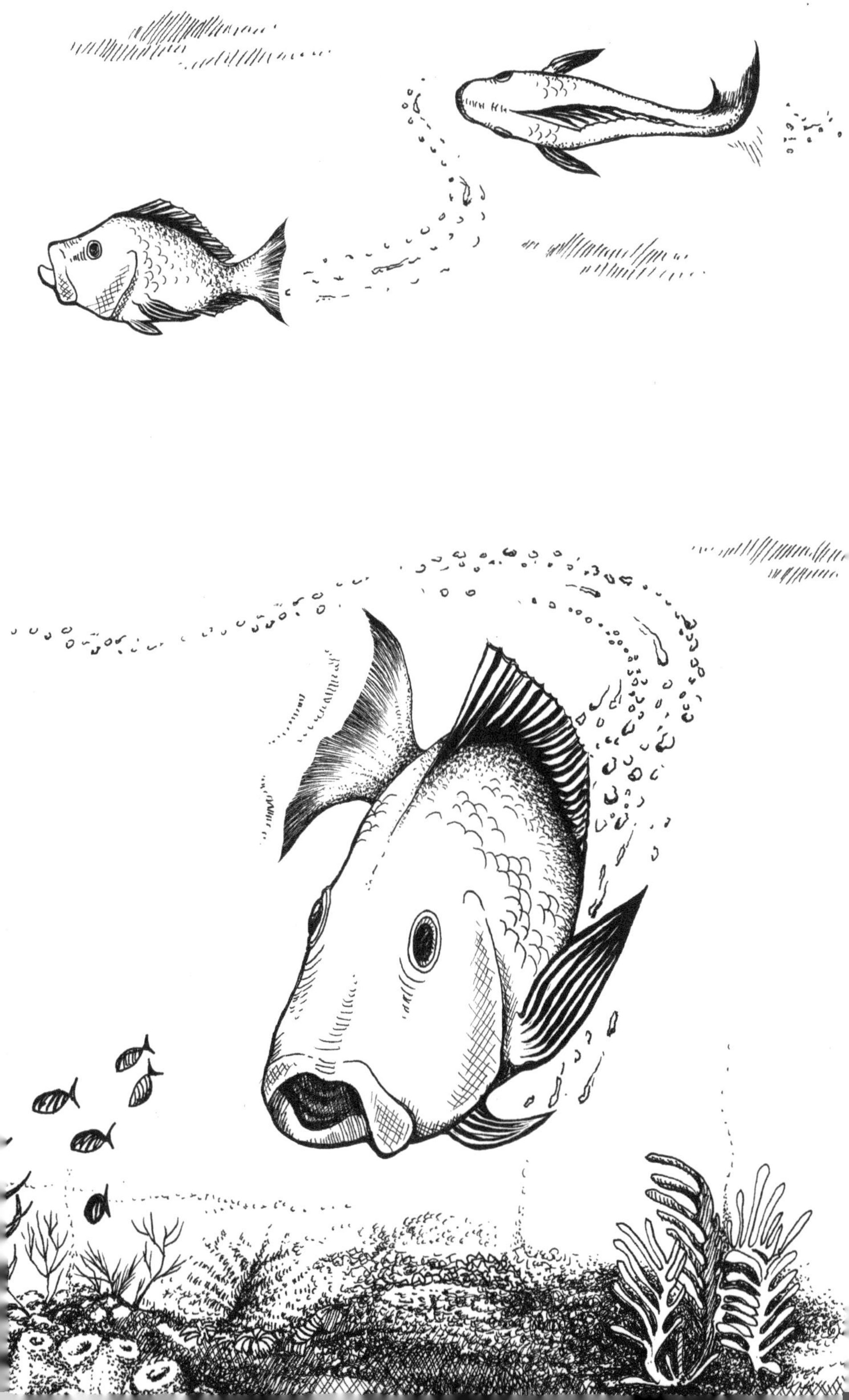

He caught up with Mike at work and told him the story. Mike didn't believe a word of it.

Bob wanted to understand what had happened, so he decided to look for help.

He told the story to a doctor but the doctor didn't believe him either.

Discouraged, Bob swam aimlessly until he came upon a sign that read "Fortune Teller".

With nowhere else to turn, Bob entered.

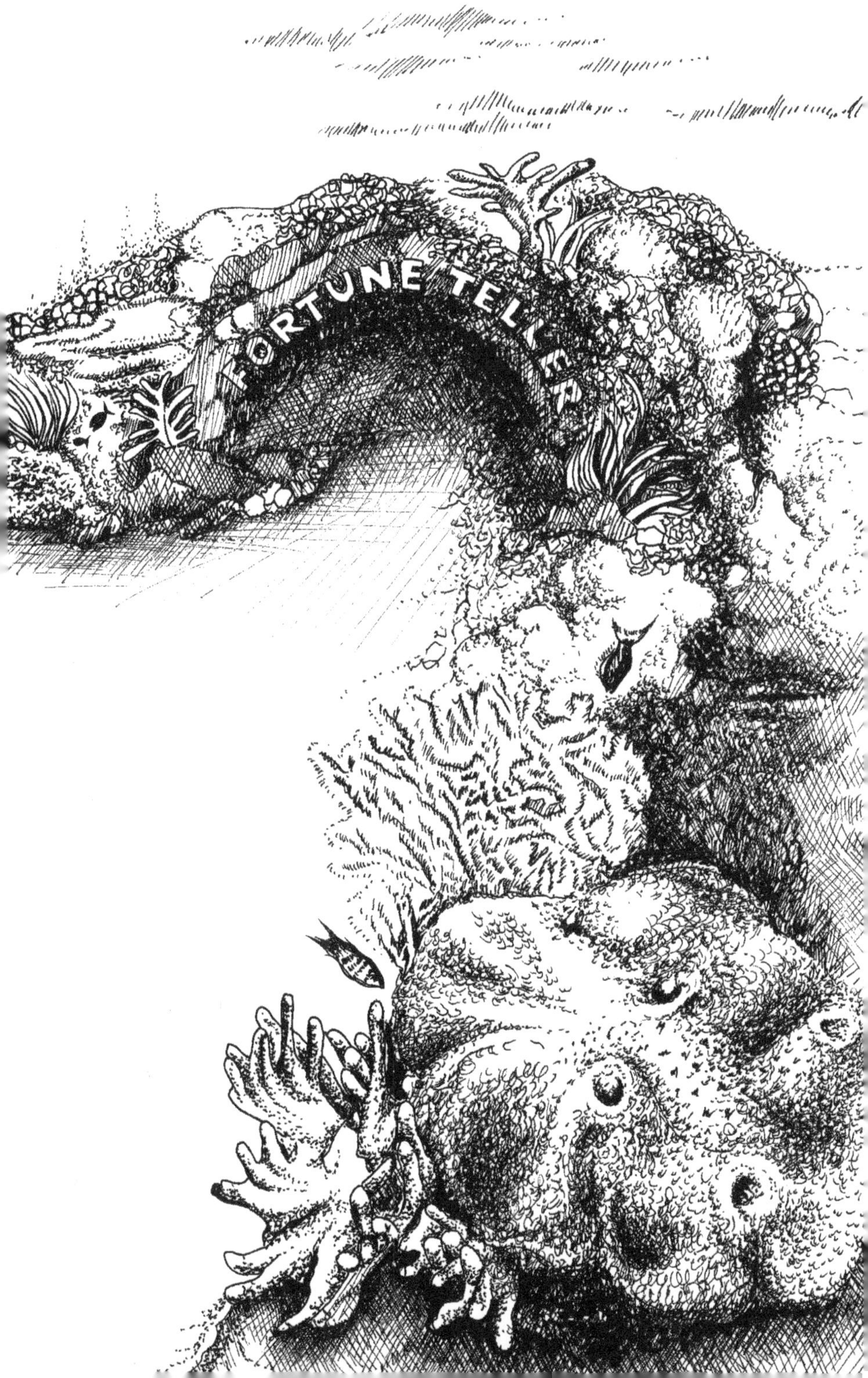
FORTUNE TELLER

He told the story to the fortune teller and she listened very intently. When Bob had finished she looked at him silently. Finally, she asked him, "How do you feel now?"

"Great," answered Bob.

The fortune teller smiled and said, "Welcome back."

Bob was confused and said, "Welcome back, where?"

"To the Ocean," she replied.

"What do you mean?" asked Bob.
"What Ocean? I don't see any Ocean?"

The fortune teller looked straight at Bob and said...

"You're swimming in it, Bob;
you're swimming in it."

As Bob heard these words tears welled up in
his eyes and one ran down his face and met
the broadest smile he had ever smiled.

23

The next day Bob had lunch with his friend Mike. The conversation, once again, turned to the Ocean. As Mike denied the Ocean's existence

Bob smiled and thought to himself...

"You're swimming in it, Mike; you're swimming in it."

The End

Special thanks to

Michael O'Keefe

...and to

The Ocean